IN WAITING

an advent devotional

FOREWORD

by Donna Hatasaki
Senior Director of Spiritual Formation

"Hope is a quiet thing that rests in the dark, gestating and nourishing the new life within, aware of the present moment and awaiting the birth of what is not yet here."

— Anonymous

This quote has sustained me lately. I find myself once again awaiting the birth of what is not yet here. Not "here" as in the world around me, but "here" as in the world within me. I find myself sitting in the dark, asking God to tend to what is quiet and nourishing within my soul, so that Christ might be fully formed in me — for the glory of God; for the abundance of my own life; and for the sake of others.

As I wait, I am reminded that waiting is not a passive activity, and I need others who are actively waiting with me. As a wise person once said, "This (inner) work is a solitary work that we cannot do alone." We need companions along The Way who are committed to doing the work required. And what work is required? It's the work of Mary. It's the work of complete surrender to God's unexpected, all-consuming, and utterly transforming love.

This set of reflections is a gift offered from a community of companions along The Way. We are pilgrims whose paths have crossed in the Good Way — a cohort offering from Learning and Leadership devoted to deepening our lives with Jesus. We are wayward children who are entirely dependent upon God's kindness and are sitting in the dark together awaiting the birth of what is not yet here. We are grateful for the privilege of actively waiting with you for Christ to be formed in us. Through his grace and by his mercy, may the Word become flesh once again.

A WORD ON WAITING

By J. Rinne

A week after Christmas many years ago, I woke up to a quiet house. The kids were still in bed, and my wife was snoozing beside me. Even the dog was napping in the living room, curled up by the fireplace. Usually, I hear her little nails clicking down the hallway as she rushes to our bed to say, "Get up!" But today, it's almost 10 a.m., and the house feels empty — like I'm the only one awake.

I'm sipping coffee, reading my Bible, and jotting down some thoughts in my journal. Through the back windows, I watch the snow gently fall on the pine trees. The pace is slow. The house is quiet. No phone buzzing in my pocket, no TV blaring in the background. Just the sounds of the house settling and the snowplows outside. Soon, I'll hear the little feet of my daughter coming up the stairs to wish me a good morning. She'll have sleepy eyes and a big hug for me. I can't wait for that, but for now, I'm savoring the stillness — the kind of moment you wish would last forever.

In the quiet, I'm reminded of the rhythm of life. Our world moves at such a fast pace — early morning practices and workouts, rushing the kids to school, a quick shower before an 8 a.m. meeting, picking up the kids, rushing them to after-school activities, then heading to a volunteer meeting or coaching event. By 11 p.m., you're crashing into bed, only to start it all over again tomorrow. Sometimes, life moves to the rhythm of a fast-paced techno song.

But here we are, nearing the end of Christmas break, and the rhythm has been slower, more like jazz music. We've been going to bed when we're tired, waking up when we're ready, eating when we're hungry, taking naps if we need them, playing outside, skiing, biking, talking, having lunch, and walking around downtown without a strict agenda. The slower pace has been a real treat.

Starting Monday, the pace will pick up again, and I've been thinking: What if this slower rhythm is more in line with how I'm meant to live? I'm not suggesting I want to sleep in every day, but what if I allowed myself time to rest, recuperate, and live in a rhythm, rather than constantly running at full speed? What if there were space in my day to sit on the couch, sip coffee, and let the Lord's voice settle into my mind and actions? What if silence, Scripture, and solitude were the first things I made time for, instead of the last things I squeeze into my busy day? What if I lived with a rhythm ordained by the Lord and directed by his Holy Spirit? What if I learned better how to wait?

But waiting can be a challenge in our world of immediacy and efficiency. In a time when productivity and multitasking are honored, and frenetic pace is the norm, I think we need to find ways to slow down.

I remember a conversation I had in the middle of the pandemic with a great friend about Psalm 23:2. She mused that maybe the Lord was "making us lie down in green pastures" to wait. Similarly, I wonder if God ordained Advent or a season of waiting because we have a hard time doing it ourselves. Like a gift that he wants to give and we need to receive. The word "Advent" comes directly from the Latin *adventus*, meaning "coming." It embodies our anticipation for what we know will arrive and represents not only the four weeks leading up to Christmas but also the centuries of waiting in hopeful anticipation for Christ's arrival.

And that is how this little book came to be. We gathered a group of friends to share reflections on this season of waiting, along with practices that might help us slow down.

So, may this Advent, this humble offering, and the practices within it be a sweet opportunity for you to connect with the God of the universe who calls you his beloved.

God's peace and blessing, J.

Table of Contents

Joy

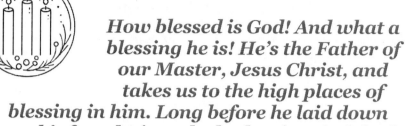

How blessed is God! And what a blessing he is! He's the Father of our Master, Jesus Christ, and takes us to the high places of blessing in him. Long before he laid down earth's foundations, he had us in mind, had settled on us as the focus of his love, to be made whole and holy by his love.
— Ephesians 1:3-4 (The Message)

From the Beginning

From the very beginning, you have been loved —not just from the beginning of your existence or the day you were born, but even before that. Before God got busy separating the night from the day, land from water, pulling up mountains, planting trees, bushes, and flowers, our Father, Papa, Jesus, and the Holy Spirit were creating a space in their hearts for you. Before they created the blueprints of Earth, the other planets, and galaxies, the focus of their attention was you.

Pause for a moment and take that in. How does it make you feel that from the very beginning, you were the focus of their love?

Now, using your imagination, place yourself in the most beautiful place you have ever been. Maybe it's the inlet at Malibu, a mountain peak in Colorado, or the aqua blue waters of the Caribbean. Whatever the scenery, place yourself in it. Sit in a spot that allows you to take in a full panoramic view. Take in all the beauty. Smell the crisp and clean air. Notice every natural thing created by God. How would you describe what you are seeing? Now, remind yourself that before he created all that you are calling beautiful, majestic, and captivating, they (Father, Son, and Spirit) weren't looking at this beautiful place and marveling at their work — they were looking at you. The word they are using is "breathtaking." They have chosen you to love, and you are the most beautiful thing they have ever laid their eyes on.

The love that was from the beginning is the same love that forms us, sets us apart, heals our wounds, and makes us whole. You were on their mind from the start, and you continue to be as you live life in this broken world. Their collective efforts in putting the world together are at work in putting us back together too.

Pause again. Where do you see God's gentleness and love at work, restoring, rebuilding, and making you whole? How does their attentive and active presence make you feel?

Application/Practice: Breath Prayer
Go back to that favorite place where you sat before.
Take a few deep breaths. Go slow.
Now, as you inhale, use a word that acknowledges their presence (e.g., Father, Jesus, Good Shepherd, Holy One, Holy Spirit, etc.).

And now, O Lord, for what do I wait? My hope is in you.
— Psalm 39:7

Hopeful Expectations

Hope is one of those things that's hard to describe, but we know it when we see it. And we certainly know it when we feel it in ourselves. At its core, hope is a sense of expectation for something to happen.

The season of Christmas is imbued with hope. For some of us (and you know who you are), we start decorating and singing Christmas songs even before Halloween. Yet, we wait until December 25 for the payoff. We wait with hopeful expectation for the big day.

However, the Bible describes hope differently. In Psalm 39:7, David says, "My hope is in you," referring to God. Jeremiah says that all of Israel will "set our hope in you, for you can do all these things." Hope is an expectation placed in something — or Someone — greater than ourselves. Hoping for presents implies that the gifts can help us in some way, but hope in the Lord is foundational to life for a believer. This kind of hope transcends our circumstances and predicaments. It's putting our trust, faith, and confidence in Someone far more powerful than anything we can ask or imagine (Ephesians 3:20).

Further, God says in his famous letter to the exiles in Jeremiah, "I know the plans I have for you … to give you a future and a hope."

Our hope — feeble, fickle, and weak as it can be — needs to be placed in the Lord. The hope he gives, which is part of our future and his plans for us, is unshakeable and trustworthy. It is, in fact, powerful.

What is your hope this Christmas? Before you answer, ask yourself: What deep desire or longing do I have for my life? Is it something related to family, friends, or work? Maybe the longing runs even deeper, reaching into our own self-understanding. Perhaps this yearning is for a better relationship, on a soul level, with the One who made you.

I encourage you to engage in the practice of reflection. Philosopher John Dewey once said, "We do not learn from experience. We learn from reflecting on experience." In a prayerful, humble posture, ask the Lord to open you up to him. Ask him to "search and know you" (Psalm 139). In doing so, he may reveal himself in your yearnings and desires.

As we wait with expectation this Advent season, let us also place our hope in God and trust that he will give us his hope — a hope fully revealed in the birth of Jesus. For he is Hope. And he is "Immanuel — God with us" (Matthew 1:23).

Application: Pray, read, reflect on this prayer. Our Father, the Author of Hope, I confess that too often my level of hope is so low that it barely registers in my life. However, your Word says that you are, in fact, our hope — not in presents or decorations, but in the Incarnation of Jesus, who is Immanuel. Whisper your hope into my heart, mind, and soul. I place my hope in you. I ask this in the strong name of Jesus, who is my hope and who is Hope. Amen.

How can it be, how can this be, that he would choose me to carry the Lord?

I Am the Lord's Servant

Mary. She is young, hidden in the routines of everyday Jewish life — until heaven breaks in and a shocking declaration is pronounced over her.

Brilliant light brings forth words: "You are highly favored. The Lord is with you" (Luke 1:28).

Notice how Mary is "greatly troubled" by these words (Luke 1:29). We might imagine her asking, "Me?"

Let's pause and imagine the Lord's presence in the room with us today, his love blinding in its intensity, ourselves as the focused delight of Almighty God. Even now, hidden as we may feel in the routines of daily life, can we, with Mary, receive the perplexing news that we too are highly favored by God on high?

The brilliant light continues, speaking words that have never been spoken before, words that stretch Mary's understanding of God, words that will shatter her reputation and any expectation of a quiet, risk-free future: "Behold, you will conceive in your womb and bear a son, and you shall name him Jesus" (Luke 1:31). The greatest mystery of all time rests on the frail shoulders of a peasant girl. And naturally, she asks, "How can this be?" (Luke 1:34).

I imagine a gasp, a furrowed brow, shortness of breath, quaking hands, searching eyes. The wonder and delight of God's favor collide with shock and confusion. Amid her conflicting emotions, she is grounded in one truth: she knows who she is. Her next words are, "I am the Lord's servant" (Luke 1:38).

I need to soak this in. Mary accepts God's reminder of who she is — highly favored. And then, though she doesn't fully understand his words, she remembers her identity as the Lord's servant. And she consents. Permission is her response, her response is one of willing surrender. Immediate, simple consent: "May your word to me be fulfilled" (Luke 1:38).

Mary amazes me. So few words in the face of massive personal upheaval, so few words in response to the immense honor of being chosen by God for a critical role in human history. She teaches me that my questions can be overshadowed by my surrender.

I'm reminded of God's words to Paul: "My power is made perfect in weakness" (2 Corinthians 12:9). Divine power was truly perfected in Mary's weakness as an unwed teenager far from the reaches of earthly esteem or privilege.

The Lord turns to me with tenderness and says, "Child, you too are my servant whom I have chosen. Remember that any other identity you value in yourself pales in comparison to this one." Can I let go of whatever privilege or control I hold, any fear or inadequacy I feel, and offer Mary's words to him today? *I am the Lord's servant.*

And as the Lord speaks to me about his plans, whether I feel baffled, afraid, or awestruck, can I consent? Can I accept my weakness and frailty as a vessel carrying the power of God? Can I invite the beautiful humility and surrender of the teenage Mary to give me hope that I too have been chosen to carry the Light of the World? Can I believe that my ordinary, everyday life — this day — has eternal implications? I don't need all my questions answered, my fears allayed, or my theology sorted. I can simply consent.

Nine months later, the baby would arrive, the mystery of all mysteries nursing at her breast, and none of Mary's words are recorded. Instead, we are told that "she treasured up all these things and pondered them in her heart" (Luke 2:19).

May we receive the grace today to embrace our identities as humble vessels carrying Christ within, servants of the reigning King, and even to boast gladly in our weaknesses, for the power of Christ rests upon us, very specifically there. May hope stir in our hearts as we welcome the Word of the Lord to be fulfilled in us. May we treasure and ponder the mystery and majesty of Emmanuel, God with us.

Application: Listen to the recording of *King of Kings* by Upperroom. It's almost 12 minutes long and offers lyrics that connect back to the Scripture we've reflected on today. Notice which lyric in particular captures your attention. Is there an invitation from the Lord?

*Wait for the Lord; be strong and
take heart and wait on the Lord.
— Psalm 27:14*

The Gift of Waiting

Near the heart of the biblical Christmas story is the expectation
that God is going to offer a gift to his people. As the story is told in
the scriptures, when those waiting finally come upon that gift, the
gift is … a newborn baby. And while I know Jesus' birth story has
been surrounded by magical imagery, sparkles, and theme music
since then, for those who had been waiting for a momentous, earth-
shattering, socio-cultural, and political revolution, the gift of a
child needing care and attention had to be at least confusing and
maybe a little disappointing. If the gift God is offering them is a
newborn, it meant having to wait again.

Then, they have to wait another 30 years before that infant grows
into adulthood and begins doing things of record.

And even then, after three more years of work with a very small
community, Jesus is arrested, and those following him have to wait
again.

After waiting through the legal proceedings, those who have been
waiting see Jesus murdered by the State (at the behest of religious
power) and have to wait again.

I don't think that process ever really ends.
I don't think the waiting ever ends.

And I've begun to wonder if the primary fruit of waiting is my
formation and becoming, rather than getting what I'm waiting for. I

wonder if waiting changes me so that I want differently (and maybe even want better).

Over time, my hopes and desires have changed. I am working to no longer expect specific results from actions or want specific gifts from God. Instead, I've begun to hope that, as I wait, my will is refined and changed.

An authentic spiritual journey has never been about grasping God or attaining some kind of personal greatness or holiness the way I'd grasp or attain an item at Walmart; it's about whole-life transformation, including the transformation of my will. One of the primary ways my will has been transformed over the years is through wanting and working for specific outcomes and not getting them (or at least not getting them the way I hoped I would while I was working at waiting). That makes tension, disappointment, and patience necessary experiences of spiritual formation. Waiting shapes me, hopefully into someone who not only wants what God is actually offering but wants God more deeply than what he's offering.

Application: Set aside some time for silent meditation or prayer focused on waiting. Begin by calming your mind and body, then reflect on what it means to wait for the Lord. Consider using a breath prayer. Once you feel settled consider any areas in your life where you feel you are waiting for God's action or direction.

Use verses like Isaiah 40:31 or Psalm 27:14 as focal points during your meditation. Visualize yourself resting in God's presence and renewing your hope and strength through that waiting.

"Every day, we cover ourselves with our own 'fig-leaf' wardrobes, seeking to prove ourselves worthy and earn a love that was always ours in the first place."
— *The God Story, Emerson and Cox*

Beloved and Beautiful

My first job out of college was teaching second grade. The surest way to get a class of 7- and 8-year-olds to sit up straight and refocus is to compliment one student out loud.

"I love the way Ryan is raising his hand to talk!" (*Everyone sits up as straight as humanly possible and reaches a hand to the sky.)

"Sally, cleaning out your desk is such a good idea!" (*Everyone begins decluttering immediately.)

"John, thank you for sharing your crayons with your neighbor." (*Mass sharing ensues.)

The inner 7-year-old in all of us longs to be chosen, noticed, and honored.

Christmastime is always special, but two Christmases in particular were memorable because I was due with two of our three sons. Anticipating the arrival of two babies during that season had a way of drawing me to Mary and her incredible, hopeful obedience. What continues to draw me in is imagining what it must have felt like to hear the angel's words found in Luke 1:28 when Mary learns she will miraculously conceive.

"Greetings, favored woman! The Lord is with you!"

The Message Bible says it like this: "Good morning! You're beautiful with God's beauty, beautiful inside and out! God be with you."

Do you find yourself sitting up a little straighter? "Pick me! Tell me I'm favored!"

Ephesians 1:5 tells us, "His unchanging plan has always been to adopt us into his own family by sending Jesus Christ to die for us. And he did this because he wanted to!"

He wanted to.

The world has a way of telling us otherwise. We are more valued when we work harder and produce more. We have to earn our seat at the table. Mistakes are unacceptable. Vulnerability makes us look weak. These are all lies that began in the garden, with the purpose of distracting us with fear and shame, ensuring we lose sight of how favored and chosen we actually are.

Application: Spend some time journaling, asking the following questions and writing down what you sense the Father has to say in response.

Father, what do you think about me?

Where am I believing lies rather than your truth?

Who else needs to hear they are favored today?

"Let him who believes in God wait for the hour that will come."

Tending the Inner Fire

By the summer of 1875, Paris was in an uproar. The art world was under siege by a rebellious band of young painters who challenged the stuffy formalism of Renaissance art. They splashed the canvas with bright colors and loose brushwork in an attempt to "paint light" and capture the "little fragments of the mirror of universal life." Their critics howled with outrage, calling these new works "absurdities" and even "crimes," accusing young radicals like Claude Monet of conducting a veritable "war on beauty."

The young Vincent van Gogh was there that riotous summer. As an aspiring artist himself, one would think that his personal correspondence (he wrote over 800 letters, most to his brother Theo) would be filled with the daily spectacle of Renoir, Degas, and other Impressionist painting passersby on the street while the horrified art community writhed with disgust. Yet not a word. Vincent's prodigious letter writing mentioned nothing of this seismic clash at the center of the art world.

Why? In short, because van Gogh had found God.

Captured by the ascetic spirituality of Thomas à Kempis, van Gogh simply eschewed the worldly trappings and glittering lights of his day. In a sense, Vincent turned dramatically inward. He followed the example of Jesus as Kempis saw him: "Withdraw your heart from the love of things visible, and turn yourself to things invisible."

Though assailed throughout his life by mental illness and social alienation, van Gogh kept the Advent hope alive that God was indeed making his presence known through him. He articulated it this way:

> There may be a great fire in our soul,
> yet no one ever comes to warm himself at it,
> and the passersby only see a wisp of smoke
> coming through the chimney and go along their way.
>
> Look here, now, what must be done?
> One must tend the inner fire, have salt in oneself,
> wait patiently yet with much impatience
> for the hour when somebody will come
> and sit down near it – maybe to stay?
>
> Let him who believes in God
> wait for the hour that will come.

Though the world clamors with cymbals and gongs, though our eyes may not be honed enough to see it, God's Kingdom is growing among us. In Christ, God's grace has been conceived in us, and it is our task, in this blessed Advent season, to "tend that inner fire." May we wait patiently, as the Virgin Mary did, for that hour to come when that seed of God's grace will be born in us. And maybe, just maybe, somebody will come, sit down near the fire of our love, and receive its warmth and light.

Application: Find a quiet space where you can sit comfortably, close your eyes, and focus on your breathing. Reflect on the metaphor of the "inner fire" and what it means to tend to it in your own life. Ask yourself what distractions you need to release to focus on nurturing your spiritual life. Write down any insights or feelings that arise during this time.

Wait, Israel, for God. Wait with Hope. Hope now; hope always!
— Eugene Peterson's version of Psalm 131

Quieting the Soul

"My heart is not proud, O Lord; my eyes are not haughty; I do not concern myself with great matters or things too wonderful for me. But I have stilled and quieted my soul; like a weaned child with its mother, like a weaned child is my soul within me. O Israel, put your hope in the Lord both now and forevermore." — Psalm 131

When I read verse two of this Psalm, I am reminded of the late-night and early-morning times with our oldest daughter when she was an infant. As a new mom trying to do everything right, I was often overwhelmed and tired. At first, when I heard her cry because she was hungry, I felt a bit of resentment; she was interrupting my sleep. However, I decided that this was a special time only she and I could share. After she was changed, fed, and full, she would fall asleep in my arms. It was quiet in our little apartment, and there was a sense of peace.

I wonder if that is what the psalmist is referring to here as we still and quiet our souls with the Lord. Is it that safe and contented feeling a baby has in its mother's arms? Do I desire to sit with the Lord and be stilled and quieted by his presence?

Something else I wonder: what must it have been like for Mary as she cared for baby Jesus? I can only imagine what that must have been like — to have him fall asleep in her arms, content, stilled, quieted. Did she also sense his peace?

As I ponder these things, I think this might be what peace could look like on a daily basis if I take the time to sit and just be with the Lord, not concerning myself with things too great or wonderful for me. To sit and bask in the peace of the Lord, the kind of peace that passes all understanding — that actually sounds quite delightful.

Application: Throughout your day, take intentional moments to pause and be present. Whether it's during your morning coffee, waiting in line, or before a meal, stop for a moment to breathe deeply, to quiet your soul and acknowledge God's presence all around you.

Use these moments to reflect on the hope that comes from resting in God's love. You might say a quick prayer of gratitude or simply savor the moment, allowing it to be a reminder of the peace that passes understanding.

"Peace I leave with you, my peace I give to you; not as the world gives do I give to you. Let not your heart be troubled, neither let it be afraid."

— John 14:27

Peace Be With You

I grew up in a Methodist Church. Every Sunday, as part of the service, we "passed the peace." In my mind, that meant going to shake hands with the people around me while mumbling, "Peace be with you." It was always awkward, particularly in junior high.

In John 14, Jesus tells the disciples that he is giving them his peace — a peace that he brought and lived during his life among us.

The Greek word is *Eirene*. It is the equivalent of the Hebrew word *shalom*. *Shalom* is a picture of life as it was meant to be. It encompasses salvation, wholeness, connectedness, righteousness, and justice. It means that we are rightly oriented in our relationships:

- Right relationship with God.
- Right relationship with one another.
- Right relationship with creation.

While the people of God were invited into *shalom*, they did not (could not) fully experience that peace. It came in smatterings, passing moments, and a few relationships. Only with the coming of Jesus could *shalom* be realized, seen, lived, and experienced. Jesus announced this shift in Matthew 4 when he began to preach, "The Kingdom of Heaven is at hand." That is to say, *shalom* is now possible.

Jesus lived life without sin, not because he never did anything wrong, but because he never broke fellowship with the Father and the Spirit. He lived every moment of every hour of every day in perfect unity with the Father and the Spirit. In doing so, he lived *shalom*. He was in right relationship with God, with those around him, and with creation.

With Advent, we remember the arrival of the ne who brought peace, lived peace, and offers peace. Advent marks the beginning of the invitation to live as Kingdom dwellers, to live *shalom*.

Jesus anticipates our response. His gifts are different. The world has no power to calm, encourage, or transform. Deep down, we are acutely aware of this reality, and we respond with distrust and fear. Before we even have a chance to process these emotions, Jesus offers a correction: Do not be afraid. Do not be troubled. What I speak is true. What I offer is *shalom*. Jesus is inviting us into the same relational existence that he lived out — perfect union with the Father, the Spirit, and himself. We can be rightly oriented to God, rightly oriented to others, and rightly oriented to the world around us. Paul echoes this charge in Philippians 4 when he writes, "Do not be anxious about anything, but in every situation, by prayer and petition, present your requests to God. And the peace of God, which transcends all understanding, will guard your hearts and minds in Christ Jesus."

Peace be with you.

Application: As a practice, take a few moments to be still. Imagine what *shalom* might look like for you today. What might it look like to be in union with God throughout your day? What might it look like to be in *shalom* with your family, your friends, your neighbors, and even your enemies? Invite the Holy Spirit to remind you of what is true throughout your day.

Glory to God in the highest heaven, and on earth peace to those on whom his favor rests.
— **Luke 2:14**

The Depth of Peace

When Matthew tells the story of Jesus' birth, he keeps it simple — no frills, just the basics. Matthew always seems focused and to the point. But Luke's telling is quite different. He spends more time on it, weaving in angels, priests, cousins, and Mary's long song of praise, joy, and surrender. He introduces characters like the shepherds, showing the collision between everyday life and a divine moment. Then there are the angels. It's as if the joy of heaven explodes onto Earth in song and praise: "Glory to God." This is God's moment, a long-planned event that will change the fortunes of humanity, bringing "peace to those on whom his favor rests." But what is peace? It often feels elusive, both in the world around us and within ourselves.

What makes the Gospel of Jesus "good news" is that it's both vast and personal. It changes things for eternity and in the present moment. On a cosmic scale, Jesus came to bring peace between us and God. Our relationship with him, once tainted and broken by our persistent desire for autonomy, is restored through Jesus' work on the cross. This is a lasting peace offered to us at a great price.

But it's hard to grasp what God's peace truly means in moments of fear and heartache. We're promised a peace that will guard our hearts and minds in Christ Jesus, but after 40 years of following him, I doubt now that it's a promise of constant tranquility. In John 14:27, Jesus says, "Peace I leave with you; my peace I give you. I do not give to you as the world gives. Do not let your hearts be troubled and do not be afraid." Preparing his disciples for incredible hardship and persecution, Jesus speaks of a peace that doesn't erase trials. For many years, I chided myself for not feeling a deep sense of calm when life spun around me. But now I wonder if my understanding of peace was a little off. Although God can certainly provide an inner sense of calm (and sometimes does), I now think of peace more as a trust — a confidence that the goodness and sovereignty of God ultimately prevail. In fact, this victory is already secured, and it's on that truth I can stand.

Living out this peace in the here and now comes from cultivating God's presence in our lives. This is what transforms our experience. It's in the daily practice of pressing into the quiet, listening to him speak to not only our minds but our hearts. If I take his words deeply to heart, they will radically change how I face life's challenges — not removing grief and sadness, but embracing them as spaces where I can feel the presence of Jesus within me.

Application: Lectio Divina. Take a moment to quiet yourself. Take a few deep breaths and become aware of God's presence all around you. Once you feel settled in, read Luke 2:1-20 one time through and look for a word or phrase that stands out to you. Read this passage again; this time focus on reading slowly and see if a new word or phrase stands out. Now read this passage a third time and ask the Holy Spirit if there is an invitation to you today from this passage. Finally, read the passage one last time and just sit quietly in gratitude to God for his living Word.

"Lord, make me an instrument of thy peace. Where there is hatred, let me sow love."
— *St. Francis of Assisi*

In the Silence, Peace Awaits

In the first chapter of Luke, we see the foretelling of the births of John the Baptist and Jesus — a prophetic baby duo! Upon receiving the news from an angel, Zechariah (John's father) is famously rendered silent for his lack of belief. Zechariah is unable to speak throughout the pregnancy and even at John's birth; it isn't until eight days after John's birth that Zechariah speaks again. With his first words, he prophesies about his son and about Jesus. Later in the chapter, Zechariah speaks directly to his son John, offering words from a father to his newborn:

"And you, my little son, will be called the prophet of the Most High, because you will prepare the way for the Lord. You will tell his people how to find salvation through forgiveness of their sins. Because of God's tender mercy, the morning light from heaven is about to break upon us, to give light to those who sit in darkness and in the shadow of death, and to guide us to the path of peace" (Luke 1:76-79 NLT, emphasis mine).

Jesus is the light who guides us to the "path of peace." He is the Good Shepherd who calls us by name and leads us to peaceful waters so that our souls might be restored. As foretold in Isaiah 9, he is the Prince of Peace.

Peace may be the most precious commodity in the world today. From political unrest at home and abroad to personal restlessness and anxiety in our own hearts, it seems we all need a greater measure of peace. Perhaps the greatest gift we can give and receive during Advent is the gift of God's peace from the Prince of Peace himself.

In order to receive the gift of God's peace, Zechariah's silence before the birth of his son may offer insight. In silence, we create space for God to speak. In silence, we stop talking and give ourselves the opportunity to listen. In silence, we let go of words to explain, justify, or rationalize, and instead, we allow God to do and say all the things we wish our words could. In silence, we trust in our heavenly Father and rest in his presence as his beloved children.

Application: As a spiritual practice today, emulate Zechariah: be silent as you go about your day. Do this for however long you wish — a few minutes, an hour, whatever feels right or is manageable for you. Refrain from talking and avoid other inputs/outputs of noise: music, podcasts, screens, singing, etc. Dedicate this silence to Jesus as you prepare to receive his peace. Whenever you feel tempted to speak, silently ask Christ to "guide you to the path of peace," as Zechariah prophesied. When your time of silence ends, commit yourself to being a person of peace in your interactions throughout the day, sharing the gift of God's peace with the world.

Let the peace of Christ rule in your hearts, since, as members of one body, you are called to peace. And always be thankful.
— Colossians 3:15

The Peaceful Pause

Advent is a season of waiting, a time for us to prepare our hearts to celebrate the coming of Christ. However, waiting can be challenging. Our world often overwhelms us with noise, distraction, and anxiety, making it difficult to wait peacefully. Yet, Advent invites us into a different kind of waiting — one rooted in peace.

Colossians 3:15 provides guidance for this peaceful waiting: "Let the peace of Christ rule in your hearts, since, as members of one body, you are called to peace. And always be thankful." The original Greek word for "rule" here, *brabeuo*, signifies "to act as an umpire." This passage encourages us to allow the peace of Christ — *shalom*, which represents a deep and abiding wholeness — to act as a referee in our lives, halting the chaos whenever peace is absent, just as an umpire pauses a game to restore order. God's peace should intervene whenever our hearts feel tumultuous, calling us back to trust and stillness.

I have experienced this deeply during a tumultuous period when my husband lost his job. We were filled with questions about our future, weighed down by financial uncertainty. As we prayed for new opportunities, waiting transformed from a simple act into a struggle as days turned into weeks and months. Anxiety crept in, and peace seemed distant.

During those moments, I reflected on Colossians 3:15, praying for God's peace to function as our referee, stepping in whenever we began to succumb to fear. I turned to a practice called centering prayer, sitting quietly with a focus on the word "trust," reminding myself to rest in God's presence. This simple act of surrendering my worries allowed the peace of Christ to act as an umpire, halting my fears and guiding me back to trust. Slowly, a profound sense of *shalom* settled within us, reminding us that God was present and at work, even when we could not see the full picture.

Looking back, I realize that embracing God's peace as the umpire in our lives did more than calm our fears; it invited us to surrender control and trust in God's timing.

During Advent, we remember how the people of Israel awaited the promised Messiah, longing for peace. Though their wait was long, God's promise was fulfilled in the birth of Christ Jesus, the Prince of Peace. As we anticipate Christmas, we are also reminded that we are awaiting Christ's return. This waiting is not meant to be filled with worry or doubt but rather with peace. Christ's peace reassures us that God is with us in our waiting, working all things for our good, even when we don't fully understand how.

To let the peace of Christ rule in our hearts means surrendering our fears and frustrations to him, trusting that he will carry us through. When peace reigns within us, it shapes our attitudes and actions, making us more patient, gentle, and thankful, even in uncertain seasons. This Advent, let us choose to wait in peace, allowing the peace of Christ to calm our hearts, guide our steps, and prepare us to receive the gift of his presence anew. In our waiting, we discover that God is already with us — *Immanuel* — and is the Prince of Peace.

Centering prayer is a form of waiting in peace because it trains us to quiet our minds and emotions and simply be with God. It cultivates an inner stillness where the peace of Christ reigns. By practicing regularly, you will find that this peace begins to extend beyond prayer time, influencing how you wait and respond to life's uncertainties. Just as Colossians 3:15 encourages us to let the peace of Christ rule in our hearts, centering prayer is a way to actively make space for that peace to settle deeply within, guiding your thoughts, emotions, and decisions, especially in times of waiting.

Application: Here's how you can engage in it:

1. **Find a quiet space:** Choose a peaceful environment where you can sit comfortably and be free of distractions.

2. **Set a time limit:** Start with 10 to 20 minutes, setting an intention to simply be with God during this time.

3. **Choose a sacred word or phrase:** Close your eyes and silently repeat your chosen word. When your mind wanders (which it will), gently return to your word without judgment or frustration.

4. **Let go and rest in God:** The goal is not to achieve any specific insight or emotion, but to rest in God's peace. Let the peace of Christ be the ruler in your heart; as thoughts or emotions arise, allow them to pass without getting caught up in them.

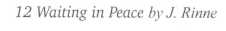

> ## *"There is no way to peace.*
> ## *Peace is the way."*
> ## *— A.J. Muste*

Peace Is the Way

It's almost Christmas day, and my whole town is alive with Christmas spirit. Christmas music fills the local shopping malls and grocery stores, lights adorn every tree in the neighborhood, and there's a noticeable lift in everyone's mood. Do you notice this too? It's one of the reasons I love the Christmas season so much. For a brief period, the world seems to embrace a certain peacefulness. Even amid the chaos of parties, engagements, shopping, and travel, there's a sense of ease that pervades the atmosphere.

Why is that? What makes this season so distinct? Why do people seem to settle in and calm down a bit more? This morning, as I dropped my son off at swim practice, I saw a sign on a building near our university campus that read, "There is no way to peace. Peace is the way." The quote struck me deeply, and I found myself pausing at the stop sign, contemplating it.

When I got home, I looked up the quote and discovered it was from A.J. Muste, a figure known as the "American Gandhi." Muste was a Calvinist preacher who evolved into a revolutionary labor leader and eventually became a radical prophet of Christian pacifism. I was intrigued by the quote and its origin, and it prompted a reflection on its meaning.

As I drove through the rainy streets of my town, I recalled something I first encountered as a child in a play, then as an adolescent in a song, and later as an adult in Holy Scripture: Jesus is called the Prince of Peace. The Bible refers to him in this way in Isaiah 9:6: "For to us a child is born, to us a son is given, and the government will be on his shoulders. And he will be called Wonderful Counselor, Mighty God, Everlasting Father, Prince of Peace."

It's clear that as we celebrate the birth of the Son of God, a profound sense of peacefulness descends upon our world. As this season reaches its peak on Christmas day, and as we transition into the New Year, may we continue to hear the peaceful rhythms of Jesus' words and actions. Let his example guide us into his Peace, his Counsel, and his Way.

Application: Take a moment to write about your feelings and experiences regarding peace during this season. Ask yourself:

- Where have I felt peace recently?
- When have I felt chaos?
- How can I invite more of Jesus' peace into my life during this season?

Spend a few moments in prayer, asking God to fill your heart with his peace. You might try the breath prayer saying something like ...

(Breathe in) "Lord, help me to recognize (pause, breathe out) your presence in my life."

(Breathe in) "May I feel the peace (pause, breathe out) that comes from knowing you."

(Breathe in) "Guide me to share (pause, breathe out) this peace with others."

*For to us a child is born,
to us a son is given;
and the government shall
be upon his shoulder,
and his name shall be called
Wonderful Counselor, Mighty God,
Everlasting Father, Prince of Peace.*

— *Isaiah 9:6*

"I think there must be something wrong with me, Linus. Christmas is coming, but I'm not happy. I don't feel the way I'm supposed to feel."

— *Charlie Brown*

Feelings and Peace

Ah, Christmas! It's an incredibly hopeful season for many. My two favorite movies of the season are *It's a Wonderful Life* and *National Lampoon's Christmas Vacation*. In both movies, the main characters have dreams — George wants to do something big and important, and Clark wants to put in a pool for his family. In each man's mind, there's a picture of what the dream fulfilled looks like, and yet it's incredibly difficult for them to grasp. They place the burden of peace on their own shoulders, but it doesn't work. Ultimately, both long for peace, and yet, no matter how hard they chase after it, their hopes are dashed, leaving them frantic and defeated.

As we journey through Advent and approach Christmas, the tension George and Clark wrestle with resonates within me.

There's a groaning for life to be at peace, and the lights, the music, and the season's festivities all stir this longing. At the same time, attempts to speed up the process and reach this perfect place only build up my anxiety and frustration, leading to "Bailey-Griswold" blowups.

Peace. The English definition of peace is described as the absence of conflict. The Hebrew word *shalom*, however, gives a fuller picture of what we were made for. *Shalom* encompasses wholeness, well-being, and the making of all things good. It's such a rich word that it defies easy definition. But *shalom* — peace in its fullest sense — is what Jesus broke into the world to bring. He came to make all things right, to restore what was broken. He will return to bring us into the fulfillment of that vision. Isaiah tells us that it's on the shoulders of the Prince of Peace — not ours.

This is the hope we live in during the Advent season. We do our best to embrace the "not right" and the "not yet," feeling our feelings while living in the hope that Jesus has completed his work on the cross and trusting that he will return to fulfill his covenant with us — *shalom* in every possible way.

Application: Examen. Take a few moments to reflect on your feelings and notice the state of your soul. Where do you feel frantic and frustrated? Where are you experiencing glimpses of *shalom*? How might God be inviting you to walk through the tension of the "not yet" while looking forward to what is and will be? Is he inviting you to release anything you've been carrying on your shoulders?

I will be with you, day after day, to the end of the age.
— *Matthew 28:20*

Jesus With Us

The question was asked, "What does Jesus mean to you in this stage of life?" It is essential to know that five couples were seated around a dinner table, all serving in full-time ministry. I sat and listened attentively for the next 15 minutes, anticipating my friends' authentic, vulnerable responses. However, with each theologically slanted response, my soul became restless. I heard each person share what they have learned about Jesus through their Scripture studies and other readings.

But repeatedly, the sharing focused on knowing Jesus, albeit with mind-blowing revelations that seemed to shift my friends' understanding of his purpose and mission both in heaven and on Earth. The more energy flowed and the more vibrant the discussion became, the more I noticed my heart and mind leaving the conversation and turning inward, as if my soul was asking for permission to come out of hiding.

When it was my turn to share, feeling a tad sweaty and emotional, I said, "What Jesus means to me in my 60s is 'with me.'" I described a season of intimacy, rest, discovery, imagination, and friendship with Immanuel — the Jesus who is with me. It is a season of drawing close to the nonjudgmental presence of my Savior and friend in silence, solitude, prayer, liturgy, poems, nature, and relationships. I shared that this "Jesus with me" season has grown my desire to be "with" another person in their pain and struggles. It has helped to silence my critical judge, who is ready to pounce on my mind and heart.

There was a collective pause, an examination of the soul, each one in their way, and then the conversation turned.

In this Advent season, where you are now, what is the meaning of "Jesus with you"?

In the opening chapter of Matthew's Gospel, Jesus is presented as the Messiah who will save his people from their sins and is called *Immanuel*, which means "God with us." Interestingly, the Gospel of Matthew ends with Jesus assuring his intimate band of friends and disciples that he will be with them always.

The narrative story of Jesus includes you — Jesus with you. Your life is bookended by your Savior and friend's merciful, loving presence. This season of Jesus with me has brought a new depth of peace that my decade of the 60s longs for.

Application: Reflect on Intimacy and Connection: Write about moments when you felt particularly close to Jesus. Describe experiences in prayer, worship, nature, or relationships that have brought you peace and a sense of his presence. You might explore how these moments have shaped your understanding of *Immanuel* or "God with us."

The father raced out to meet him, swept him up in his arms, hugged him dearly, and kissed him over and over with tender love.
— *Luke 15:20 (TPT)*

The Father Who Pursues

I recently gave a talk on Luke 15, best known as the Parable of the Prodigal Son. This was how I had always known it. However, I then realized it is a parable of two sons, not just one, and both were lost. So, I began to call it the Parable of the Two Lost Sons. But it wasn't until I read Timothy Keller's book called *The Prodigal God* that I discovered the best title for this parable. It truly is a Parable of the Prodigal God. The definition of the word "prodigal" is "recklessly extravagant." Through this parable, Jesus describes what his Father is like — he is the recklessly extravagant Father who loves his creation with a reckless, extravagant love.

As I prepared for this talk, the further I dug, the more I discovered.

Luke 15:20: "And he got up and came to his father. But while he was still a long way off, his father saw him and ran and embraced him and kissed him."

Luke 15:28: "But he became angry and was not willing to go in; and his father came out and began entreating him."

Did you catch it? Yeah, it took me several readings too before it clicked. The father went out to both sons. He pursued them; they did not pursue him! This Prodigal Father that Jesus wants us to know is not only recklessly extravagant with his love; he pursues his beloved creation.

Eric Peterson, at his father Eugene Peterson's memorial service, said his dad had only four main thoughts from which all of his sermons sprang:

1. God loves you.
2. He's on your side.
3. He's coming after you.
4. He's relentless.

Sounds like the pursuing Prodigal Father, doesn't it?!

Application: During this Advent season, take some time to engage in the practice of Lectio Divina over Luke 15:1-32. If you are able, place yourself in the position of both sons. What do you experience as you encounter the pursuing, recklessly extravagant love of the Father? What does his embrace, like the one he gave to the younger son, feel like to you? How do you respond to his invitation to the older son, filled with deep inner resentments, to come in and join the party in the Father's home?

As the Quakers were often known to say, "May you be seized by the power of a great affection" for you as you engage in this passage.

"We are not what we have. We are not what we do. We are not what other people say about us. We are the beloved."
— *Henri Nouwen*

From Oblivion to Awareness

I can't believe I'm actually saying this but I miss the pandemic. Well, part of it at least. It forced me to hunker down to a degree that I never would have chosen were it not for the devastation of that inimical little virus. I would have just kept on going. Frenzied workloads and frantic activity, all driven by this invisible pressure, both within and without, to hurry up, move fast, do more, don't look back. The pandemic forced me to stop, to simplify, to strip it down to the bare essentials. I loved that. My kids loved that. Now that the pandemic has eased, it seems like I'm right back where I started and my soul is buckling under the burden.

St. Paul rings the alert, "It is the hour now for you to awake from sleep … the night is advanced, the day is at hand" (Romans 13:11). Some translations read, "Time is running out. Wake up!" My favorite paraphrase is, "Make sure that you don't get so absorbed and exhausted in taking care of all your day-by-day obligations that you lose track of the time and doze off, oblivious to God." I've learned that it's easy to get so absorbed and exhausted by life that my spiritual life dozes off. I become oblivious to God.

Distracted. Heedless. Preoccupied. Zonked. All of these are synonyms for the word "oblivious" and I'm guilty of them all. I'm not consciously denying God, I'm just drifting, absorbed and exhausted in the ever-urgent day-to-day. The Lord says, "Stay awake!" Don't drift. Stay the course. Don't fall right back into the trap of a distracted and disintegrated life.

Sometimes I wonder if God gave us the season of Advent because he knew full-well what we would eventually make of Christmas — the christening of consumerism, the elevation of material excess, and the blinding blur of busyness. The Savior of the world comes and we're all out to lunch.

As we're preoccupied by our own frenetic activity, God gives us a baby, born of a humble teenager, in the silence of the night, claiming nothing for himself but his own dependence on Mary and Joseph. God's power loves silently and without coercion. God loves us through a precious baby and gently beckons us to love him in return.

This Advent, God waits for us to wake up from our slumber and gaze at him gazing at us. Perhaps opt for a quiet night at home instead of one more dinner party? Something tells me we'd be happier. Maybe give our children the gift of *presence* this year instead of presents? Something tells me they'd be happier. Maybe turn off the endless chatter of the television, make a nice cup of hot chocolate, and sit in the silence of God? Gosh, that sounds nice.

Advent is a time for us to wake up, hunker down, and overcome our spiritual oblivion. We shouldn't need another pandemic for that. What do you need to rise out of oblivion and into the invigorating waters of God's love?

Application: Read Luke 2:1-20 or Isaiah 9:6-7 slowly and ask yourself a few reflective questions:

- How is God inviting me to wake up from spiritual oblivion during this season?
- What does it mean to me that God came as a humble baby?
- How can I cultivate more presence in my daily life?

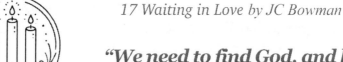

"We need to find God, and he cannot be found in noise and restlessness. God is the friend of silence."
— *Mother Teresa*

Righteous Waiting

I enjoy movies, and that is putting it lightly. I love a good story and seeing how the characters interact. I am fascinated by the angles the director chooses to shoot a scene and appreciate how the supporting characters help move the plot from one moment to the next as the story unfolds. The supporting actors and actresses are crucial in holding the story together.

In Scripture, the supporting characters are essential. Many appear in only a few verses, but they have an incredible impact on Salvation History. One of my favorites is Simeon, who shows up in the book of Luke 2:25-35 (take a moment to read it if you can).

Simeon is described as "righteous and devout." Wouldn't you like that on your gravestone? He lived an integrated life. What he practiced in the quiet of his soul (devotion) he lived out among the people he interacted with. In other words, he lived out what he believed.

At some point in his life, Simeon was told he would get to see the Messiah before he died. I can't imagine how he felt to have this revealed to him. The Jewish people had been waiting for thousands of years for the Lord to bring Israel the Messiah, the One who was to rescue God's chosen people, and Simeon knew that he would see the One they had all been waiting for. Did he feel hopeful, prideful, expectant, impatient, anxious, or peaceful? I guess he felt all this and more, but he never wavered in his trust in the Lord's word. Simeon was "devout and righteous." In his trust, he waited with expectant patience and listened. He had to be quiet and recognize the Lord's voice to truly hear him.

I don't know if you are like me, but being quiet is hard. I am surrounded by noise — people, traffic, radio, TV, phones, and computers — all drowning out the voice I need to pay attention to. Simeon knew to be quiet and recognized the voice of the Lord as he was prompted to go to the Temple, where he found the baby Jesus being held by his mother. It was there that Simeon declared Jesus the Messiah for all people, both Jews and Gentiles alike.

Simeon teaches me to live an integrated life — a life that trusts the Lord, waits expectantly, and learns to be quiet enough to recognize the voice of the Lord. I want to live a life that is obedient to that voice because I know it will always lead me to Jesus.

By the way, the name Simeon means "one who hears."

Application: Spend time in nature, intentionally quieting your mind and allowing space for contemplation. Maybe this is in the hills, your neighborhood, or on a snowy peak. As you walk, reflect on the ways God speaks through his creation and consider how you can better recognize his voice in your life.

Listening Prayer: Engage in a form of prayer where you spend time not just talking to God but also listening for his response. After sharing your thoughts and feelings, take a few moments of silence to see if God brings anything to your mind or heart.

Mary consoles Eve.

An Encounter With Eve and Mary

Begin by finding a journal to record your thoughts. Place both feet flat on the floor, close your eyes, and take a moment to relax. Breathe in and out slowly several times.

Now, open your eyes and gaze at the image before you. Take in the entire picture, noticing the shapes, colors, and lighting. Pay attention to the details in both the foreground and background.

Once you have visually surveyed the artwork, allow yourself to enter into it. This is a sacred invitation from God, drawing you toward a treasure meant just for you.

Consider the arch formed by the wood and branches of the tree, alongside the wood of the cross. The arch plays a significant role in both architecture and art, symbolizing strength and support, lightness and openness amidst density, as well as beginnings and endings. In mythology, arches or doorways represent thresholds — transitions between the temporal world (chronos) and the spiritual realm (kairos).

Next, notice the yellow-gold light enveloping this scene. This color often represents the presence of the divine, signifying God's Holy Spirit as it enfolds and caresses both Eve and Mary.

As you reflect, read Genesis 2:19-3:24.

Consider how you find yourself as Eve approaching Mary, who is pregnant with the Son of the Most Holy God — our salvation.

In your imagination, take a moment to feel the serpent's body coiling around your leg. Have you experienced the constriction of the enemy's slimy and deceptive power? What specific situations in your life have made you feel strangled? What currently threatens to wrap around you? Allow any emotions that arise as you consider how you have been ensnared by the enemy.

Feel the fruit in your hand, grasping it close to your body. How have you attempted to control your life outside of God's provision and power?

As you feel the fig leaves around your waist, reflect on how you might be hiding from the truth. In what ways have you refused to acknowledge your human frailties, instead crafting a façade for the world? What do you manipulate or use to present an image of yourself to those around you?

Can you identify with the look of shame on Eve's face?

What additional emotions surface as you ponder these questions? Speak to Jesus, the lover of your soul, about your feelings, and look for his compassionate and loving gaze upon you.

Mary takes your hand and places it gently on her belly, where Jesus — fully God and fully man — is being knit together in her womb. Take a few moments in this sacred space. How does it feel to have Eve place your hand on her belly? Do you welcome this gesture, or does it feel threatening?

What is it like to meet Mary's understanding and compassionate gaze? What does her look communicate about Jesus' heart? Is there anything you wish to express to Jesus in this moment?

Feel Mary's hand on your face as she lifts your head. What emotions rise within you?

You may sense the coils of the serpent loosening around your legs, realizing that the serpent has been crushed (Genesis 3:15). Talk to Jesus about this transformation.

What implications does the life growing within Mary hold for you? Is there something you want to ask God or seek from him in this place? What is your deepest need from him? He meets your gaze, inviting you to express your heart.

Now, simply rest in his presence — the One who loves you beyond measure. Savor the stillness, and let his love soothe you.

"Mary and Eve" used with permission from Sister Grace Remington, OCSO. Crayon and Pencil. c.2005, Sisters of the Mississippi Abbey https://mississippiabbey.org/

Love is patient and kind; love does not envy or boast; it is not arrogant or rude. It does not insist on its own way; it is not irritable or resentful; it does not rejoice at wrongdoing, but rejoices with the truth. Love bears all things, believes all things, hopes all things, endures all things. Love never ends.

— 1 Corinthians 13:4-8

His Love Never Ends

Known as "The Love Chapter," 1 Corinthians 13 offers us a truly wonderful and inspiring language of love on the topic of Christian love. These words are not only meant to be read and heard at the beginning of a marriage but are words for our daily walk with Jesus. They are also connected with Christmas.

Because of their familiarity, let's take a fresh look with an open heart. First, notice that this description and definition of love is balanced. There are eight positive things and eight negative things. Putting them into columns can give us a better look:

What Love Is	What Love Isn't
Patient	Envious
Kind	Boastful
Rejoices in truth	Arrogant
Bears all things	Rude
Believes all things	Insistent on its own way
Hopes all things	Irritable
Endures all things	Resentful
Never ends	Rejoices in wrongdoing

Now, imagine these two columns as opposite banks of a river. Unlike real river travel, our goal is to stay closer to one bank over the other. On one bank is Love: the conditions are calm, gentle, sunny but not hot. There is a steady current, but not rough. Pleasant.

The other bank is What Love Is Not: dark and rough conditions, with rapids appearing out of nowhere. A current that is raging, pushing us both downstream and in circles at the same time. Chaotic.

Remember, our goal is to stay on one side rather than the other. However, even with our best intentions, from time to time, we drift across this river; we lose sight of ourselves and how we are acting. Maybe a twinge of arrogance tells us that we can take a small step away from the bank of Love and venture out more into the middle on our own. Or we come across someone who is unlovable and causes our emotions to twist just by being in their presence. Whatever the case may be, we drift into the dark and stormy waters of the other bank.

This is why Jesus came in the first place. His is the Voice on the Bank of Love that calls us back to him. For at Christmas, our Caller was born to save us not only from the wrong side of the river but to continually call us to his bank.

"For God so loved, he gave ..." (John 3:16). In terms of Jesus' birth, God gave. He invaded reality, history, and our circumstances; He "moved into the neighborhood" and into relationships — into our hearts.

"God is love" (1 John 4:8). And because Jesus is God, then Jesus too is love. His love for us was self-sacrificial. He too gave. Ultimately, He gave on the cross — the True Gift for us all. And if we are to spend our lives becoming more like Jesus, we too are to love self-sacrificially.

How do we do that? By being patient and kind. Rejoicing in truth. Bearing, believing, hoping, and enduring in all things.
And when we are not — and of course, there will be times when we are not — we need to ask for forgiveness, repent, and try again. Jesus, the incarnate Word of God, who was born of Mary in a barn, is right now calling us back to himself.
To his side of the river.
His love ... never ends.

Most Holy and Gracious God, love is such a force that it plays out in thousands of different ways in our lives. We are so prone to drift from your definition of love in 1 Corinthians 13. We want to define it for ourselves. We want to manipulate love to serve our own needs.

Father, convict us of this; correct us of this. Reorient us to your definition and example of love as seen in Jesus' life, death, and resurrection. May we, in this season of love, become more like him as we humble ourselves to love others as you love them. Thank you for your incredible love for us. In Jesus' name, we pray, Amen.

Application: Reflect on the Banks

Picture the "Bank of Love" on one side of the river. Picture the qualities of love there — patience, kindness, truth, and hope. Let yourself rest on this side of the river. On the other side, see the characteristics that love avoids — envy, pride, irritability, and resentment. Let these stay on the opposite bank, away from you.

Now take a moment to reflect on times in recent days when you may have drifted away from love's bank, even briefly. Perhaps you felt impatient or frustrated, or maybe pride got in the way. With a gentle heart, ask God for forgiveness for these moments and for help in realigning yourself with his love.

Next, picture Jesus standing on the Bank of Love, calling you back whenever you stray. As you breathe deeply, hear him speak words of encouragement and love, guiding you toward patience, kindness, and endurance. Let his voice remind you that love's path is always open to you.

Now, think about one quality of love you would like to embody today — maybe kindness, patience, or endurance. Set an intention to focus on this quality throughout the day. Ask God to help you live it out, especially in moments when it's difficult.

Finish with a prayer, thanking God for his unwavering love and presence. Ask for strength to stay close to love's bank, and invite the Holy Spirit to guide you back when you start to drift.

We cannot wait till the world is sane to raise our songs with joyful voice, for to share our grief, to touch our pain, He came with Love: Rejoice Rejoice!
— Madeline L'Engle

Abundant Joy - John 2: 1-12

A wedding. The bride, the groom, Aunt Margaret, and Uncle Fred. Everyone in town has gathered for this feast in Cana — a celebration meticulously planned and dreamt of, likely since the bride and groom were children. It's more than just a day of joy; it's the uniting of two families and the exchange of lifelong promises.

In the midst of the festivities — dancing, laughter, and the glowing smiles of the newlyweds — a problem emerges. The wine is gone. The whispers start. *"What happened to the wine? Check again. Maybe there are extra bottles in the storage room. Who did the math? Was it stolen?"* The rumors ripple among the servants.

Wine, much like the wedding chuppah or the breaking of a glass, holds deep significance at a Jewish wedding. Wine represents the collective **joy** of all the participants that this day has arrived. It's with **joy** that the host shares the wine with all the event-goers. It's with **joy** that the couple celebrates their parents, who have led them to this day, as they drink wine poured by their in-laws. To run out of wine at such an occasion is more than a logistical hiccup — it's a cultural embarrassment, something that would be gossiped about for years to come.

So when Mary says, *"They have no more wine,"* in verse three, it's not just an observation; it's an expression of empathy. She knows the social disaster looming for the newlyweds and their families — the whispers, the smirks, the wedding remembered not for its joy, but for its failure. The bride and groom would carry the shame, the story recounted in their small town.

As Mary sits at this wedding, she likely remembers her own story from thirty years ago. Mary surely recalls her dreams of her own wedding, with friends and family, with dancing and wine. The time she would wear the veil and say her vows. The dream overshadowed by an unexpected pregnancy. As Mary's belly grew, so did the rumors. The wedding she had dreamed of was set aside as she embraced the unexpected reality God had for her.

So when Mary looks into Jesus' eyes and says, *"They have no more wine,"* there's a depth to her words. She knows embarrassment. She knows shame and the burden of whispered gossip. Jesus sees her and knows her. He knows her past just as he knows ours. He knows the dreams Mary relinquished, and all she carried so that she could carry Jesus into this moment.

Then Jesus does what he always does — he gets involved. As he steps into his public ministry, he begins with a powerful act of redemption. From simple foot-washing water, he creates abundant wine as a symbol of abundant joy. Not just any wine, but the best.

A miracle is done for everyone present — for the bride and groom, their families, the servants, the disciples, and definitely for Mary. It is a sign of all that Jesus has come to redeem and how he transforms the ordinary into extraordinary joy.

May we have eyes to see the endless joy he offers, and may we trust in his power to redeem all things. May we celebrate as if we are at a good friend's wedding.

Application: Take some time to reflect and consider creating something to represent joy. Maybe paint or draw; maybe write a poem or a letter to God. Reflection Questions:

- What have you lost? What dreams did you plan and prepare for that never materialized?
- Where has God brought unexpected joy into your life?
- How can you celebrate God's joy today?

Fear not, for behold, I bring you good news of a great joy!
— *Luke 2:10*

"We should, to begin with, think that God leads a very interesting life, and that he is full of joy. Undoubtedly he is the most joyous being in the universe."
—*Dallas Willard*

The Christmas Shepherd

Have you ever wondered why the angels were first sent to *shepherds* to announce Jesus' birth? I mean ... instead they could have rounded up all the higher-ups in Palestine for a massive press conference to welcome in the King of Kings, right? But no ... they were sent to proclaim the most game-changing event (OF ALL TIME) to lowly shepherds who were just doing their normal sheep-herding gig on a hillside next to Bethlehem.

I don't know ... but maybe it has to do precisely with the simple fact that they were shepherds. Nothing more, nothing less. That is, their vocation was a beautiful sign pointing to the arrival of God as THE Shepherd of his people. This metaphor (that we are like sheep to God as our shepherd) is one of the most frequently used relational metaphors in the Bible. It's somewhere around 118 verses. Now, fast forward 30 years and Jesus boldly claims that *he is* God as our shepherd when he says, "I am the good shepherd ...

My sheep hear my voice and I know them, and they follow me" (John 10:11, 27).

Isn't this what we all so deeply desire? That we would **hear the voice of the God who loves us and calls us his own.** So amidst all the demanding, fearful, and anxious voices that may be creeping up on us this season … may we press back instead, receiving this great joyful news: The Good Shepherd has come and he calls us to come close because we belong to him.

Application: Find a quiet place and set a five-minute timer to just sit still and repeat the breath prayer: *"Lord Jesus, you are my good shepherd and I belong to you."*

"In our society, there is a lot of talk about the need for action. But it is in solitude that we can learn how to listen and how to be with others."
— *Henri Nouwen*

Hurry?

American psychologists once conducted a fascinating experiment on a group of seminary students. They settled these well-meaning young students in a room at the end of a large hospital and told them they were participating in an experiment on verbal retention. Each student would be invited individually into a room where a psychologist would read a variety of Bible passages. Afterward, they would be instructed to walk down a long corridor to the other end of the hospital, where they would be asked to repeat what they had heard.

Half of the students listened to random passages from the Bible, while the other half heard the parable of the Good Samaritan (the one where a man was beaten and left broken on the side of the road, and only the Samaritan stopped to help while the other "religious types" passed by). What these students weren't told was that researchers had stationed a man in an alcove of the hallway, lying on the ground and looking battered, just like the man in the parable. Would they stop to help? Would those students who had just heard the parable of the Good Samaritan be more likely to stop?

Researchers were amazed by the results. Some students did stop, but there was no significant difference between the two groups. What astounded them even more was the effect of one simple word added to the instructions before sending these theology students down the hall: hurry. When they were told to hurry, not one student stopped to help the battered prop, even those who had just heard the Gospel passage encouraging them to do so. Not one.

It seems that hurry blinds us. Even when we genuinely care, even when we want to do the right thing, hurry blurs our vision and prevents us from seeing Jesus right there in front of us, disguised in the lonely, the forgotten, and the passed-over.

How might you take the time this Advent to slow down and open your eyes to the world around you? You might just be surprised by what you've been missing.

Application: Take an intentional walk.

Set an Intention: You might focus on being present, noticing the beauty around you, or being open to seeing others in need.

Begin with Awareness: Notice the sensation of your feet connecting with the earth and the rhythm of your breath.

Engage Your Senses: As you walk, engage your senses fully. Notice the sights, sounds, and smells around you. What do you see? Are there colors or shapes that stand out? Can you hear birds chirping, leaves rustling, or distant laughter?

Practice Gratitude: With each step, reflect on something you're grateful for.

Notice Others: Are there individuals who seem in need of help or companionship? Perhaps someone who looks lost or in distress? Allow yourself to pause and consider how you might offer assistance, even if it's just a smile or a kind word.

Conclude with Reflection: How did it feel to slow down and be present? Did you notice anything new or different about your surroundings?

> ## *"Restore to me the joy of your salvation, and uphold me with a willing spirit."*
> ### *— Psalm 51:12*

"I have a heart with room for every JOY."
— Phillip James Bailey

Joyful Celebrations

Last night, as I was tucking my daughter into bed, she said, "Dad, it's almost Christmas Eve … wait, actually, it's pre-pre-Christmas Eve." I chuckled a bit, said some bedtime prayers, and then headed upstairs to retire for the evening. Sometimes, as an adult, I can get a bit jaded with things, even with the big stuff like the Advent season. So, I was really touched by my daughter's simple and profound excitement for this season. She was so enthusiastic that she even coined the term "pre-pre-Christmas Eve." How are you feeling this Advent season?

You might be feeling a bit bored, a bit old, or a bit unexcited in the waiting. Maybe you could consider the posture of "Waiting with Joy" like my daughter taught me to do. What if you took a page from my daughter's book and celebrate a "pre-pre-Christmas Eve" in your own way. It could be a pre-game celebration of your favorite football team, a celebration with your toes in the ocean, or maybe even celebrating a family member visiting you for the season. Or it could simply be a moment to stop and thank God for the little things in life.

In closing, I often end birthday wishes to my friends and family with, "Celebrate well, you deserve it." I hope that you can believe that today and engage it and celebrate well.

Application: Today, find something to be excited about, thank the Lord for it, throw a little party because of it, tell someone you love them just because, or just be joyful. Additionally, you can try one or two of these practices today. Think of them like you're trying on a new shirt or pair of pants. See how they fit and if you like them.

Joyful Waiting: During times of waiting — like waiting in line or waiting for a holiday gathering — turn those moments into prayer time. Use the opportunity to meditate on the joy of Advent and the hope of Christ's birth, allowing those thoughts to fill you with peace and anticipation.

Acts of Kindness: Find small ways to spread joy in your community. Whether it's helping a neighbor, volunteering, or simply offering a smile to someone in need, these acts can be powerful reminders of God's love and grace working through you.

Mindful Moments: Schedule quiet moments throughout your day to pause and reflect. During these moments, take a few deep breaths, center your thoughts on God, and invite his joy into your heart. Use this time to listen for his guidance or simply enjoy his presence.

Celebrate the Little Things: Throughout Advent, intentionally highlight and celebrate the small moments of joy in your life. This could be through simple rituals like lighting a candle at dinner or sharing a joyful memory with loved ones, reminding you of God's presence in the everyday.

I bring you good news that will bring great joy to all people. The Savior—yes, the Messiah, the Lord.
— *Luke 2:10-11*

Sharing Sacred Experiences

Recall a time when you experienced deep goodness and beauty and shared the glory of that moment with others.

Perhaps it was an autumn drive in the mountains with friends, surrounded by the golden glow of aspen trees at sunset. A cool breeze balances the warmth of the sun's rays. The perfect song plays, and you hear someone say, "Turn it up!"

Or maybe it was a quiet December morning. You plug in the Christmas tree, wrap yourself in a blanket, and savor your first cup of coffee, greeting the day enveloped in a peace that is nearly palpable.

Consider a holiday meal — special flavors and traditions shared with loved ones on a meaningful day.

These are sacred times and spaces where heaven draws near and God's glory shines around us. Like the heavenly choir that filled the Christmas night sky with praise, our glory-filled moments can remind us of the joyful news that God is with us, that unto us a Savior has been born. Like the shepherds, our awestruck hearts can prompt us to run and see if the promises of God are true. And when we've tasted and seen this goodness for ourselves, we want others to know this joy, too.

This is the heart of the ministry of Young Life — our staff and volunteer leaders embody an answer to adolescents who ask, "Where is God? Does he see me? Does he even care?" Our incarnational presence shouts, "YES! He is here! He loves you! He gave everything so he could be in relationship with you!" Young Life is a hallelujah chorus in high resolution, pointed directly at the hearts of kids!

This Advent, may we receive afresh the good news that has been, and continues to be, announced over us! May we sense God's glory and beauty all around. May we be enlivened to taste and see for ourselves that God's promises are good and true, and may we find ourselves sharing the source of our joy with those around us. Joy to the world, ad infinitum!

Application: Visio Divina

Take a moment to gaze upon Daniel Bonnell's painting, "Seeing Shepherds." The artist says, "This painting was inspired by the Scripture that describes how a myriad of angels appeared to the humble shepherds in the fields. How would that have appeared to the shepherds? You, the viewer, are in the painting; you stand amongst the sheep."

Consider the following questions:

1. What thoughts or emotions might this painting be stirring up within you?

2. What do you notice about your heart's posture as you contemplate this image? Does it usher you into an attitude of prayer? If so, let these prayers take form in you. Write them down if you wish.

3. You may choose to close your time by offering your prayers to God in a moment of silence.

> ### *The light shines in the darkness, and the darkness has not overcome it.*
> ### *— John 1:5*

A Light in the Darkness

Do you know why December 25th was chosen as the date to celebrate Jesus' birth? One theory is that the Winter Solstice, attributed to this day, is linked to the darkest day in the middle of winter. It is the darkest time of the year, and being in the heart of winter places us furthest from the fall harvest and from springtime's new growth. Depending on where and when you live in history, you might need to consider how to avoid starving or freezing to death during this time of year.

Wisdom won the day when this date was chosen. At the darkest, coldest, and most anxiety-producing time of the year, we celebrate the Light of life. We celebrate the warmth of the Father's embrace. We rest in the Peace on Earth that only our Savior can bring.

Merry Christmas! I pray you are blessed with memory after memory of the Lord's peace and goodness, even in your own Winter Solstice. God is Light.

Application: Please take a moment to consider this question in a journal entry or during a walk: Where have you experienced the Lord's peace lately? Where have you encountered chaos? What might the Lord be inviting you into based on your answers?

Made in United States
Cleveland, OH
27 November 2024

10987558R00037